UPSTATE

THE WESLEYAN POETRY PROGRAM: VOLUME 55

UPSTATE

By DUGAN GILMAN

'Now', says you, 'that door exists, as plain as if I saw it.
There's nothing else remains to be done but to find it!'
—Mole to Ratty,
The Wind in the Willows

WESLEYAN UNIVERSITY PRESS
Middletown, Connecticut

Some of these poems have previously appeared elsewhere. For permission to reprint, and for the assignment of copyrights, the author is grateful to the editors and publishers of the following:

Alkahest: American College Poetry; Chicago Review; Epoch; From Out of the Salt Mound Anthology; Hudson Review; Nickel Review; Poetry Northwest; The Salt Well; Syracuse Poems 1968; Tennessee Poetry Journal; and *TransPacific.*

"After Eating Salt Fish" was first published in *Poetry.*

"Words Entrusted to the Flanks of a White Doe I Almost Hit where Three Roads Meet near Delphi, N.Y." was first published in *Malahat Review.*

Paperback: ISBN: 0-8195-1055-6

Hardbound: ISBN: 0-8195-2055-1

Library of Congress Catalog Card Number: 79-142724

Manufactured in the United States of America

FIRST EDITION

To Emmie

CONTENTS

Han-Shan & Shih-Te Climb a Back Fence in Syracuse, N.Y. [11]

So This Is the End of the World [12]

Once [13]

Gleaners [14]

Californium [15]

Libation [16]

Lebensraum [17]

Family Reunion with Ghosts at New York Harbor [18]

A Bucket Kicked Aside in Memory of Those Few Who Must Yet Die to Make Cowardice a Unanimity [20]

Working on the Erie Canal: Some Last Frontiers [21]

Bog [28]

When I Am Old [29]

February [30]

Two Fire Festivals [31]

    For My Wife, Because I Forgot to Get Her a Valentine

    Midsummer

Greeting the First March Wind with a Hangover [32]

Spring Fever [33]

How We Hang onto Those Floating Ribs [34]

How Dry I Am [35]

Cellarhole [36]

After Eating Salt Fish [37]

The Wild Wood [38]

Summons [39]

Words Entrusted to the Flanks of a White Doe I
Almost Hit Where Three Roads Meet near
Delphi, N.Y. [40]

An Aside [42]

Labor Hall of Fame [43]

Legs of a Poor Man's March on Resurrection
City [44]

Returning [48]

Water Witches [49]

Remembering You [50]

Upstate [51]

This Past Summer [52]

Trail's End [53]

Dew Line [54]

The Pear Tree [55]

October [56]

Looking for Snow [57]

Arbor Day, in the Winter of Family Trees [58]

Elms [60]

Black River Country [61]

Dry Run [62]

The Vanishing Point [63]

The Home in Dead Weeds [64]

UPSTATE

Landing feet first in the back lot
like two ragged lunatics that night,
who suspected pterodactyls to be flying
underground? We prowled for rabbit tracks.
West of branches thrown from neighbors' yards
in mounds, the new snow bellied toward the moon,
a ginko tree's long shadow lay like water
waiting just for us: two hundred million years.
How could we've possibly explained ourselves,
craned up at a moon full of our own footprints,
yet so clear we could still see the ocean beds
waiting for the tide, in Pre-Pacific time.

In a moment, we just had to break out laughing
at some flakes sifted gently from a bough; —
you too had just noticed the flashlights
skittered silently along the fence.

We have crossed the seas of darkness.
We have reached that gelatinous edge
where asphalt slops over the side
of the flat earth, behind a body shop.
We have heard the slush knocking
at the hulls of junked autos swamped & gutted,
left to face upstream forever
beneath the night-fished stars.
We have gone too far.
Yet the moon just met me in a shattered windshield.
It is a fleece; it is something golden in me
that is saved, kept secret, in these Christless times.

Once,
when the sun had been loaded
early on the boat, the keelman
turned to pet the horses.
His hand finding nothing
but the dark, he shoved off;
and said nothing to the rowers
for one whole hour,
for fear he had been asleep.

Often,
at the harvest of a heavy bender,
it is still dark.
My drinking arm,
old scythe of many snow-searched barley fields,
is relaxed. And so I get up on my hind legs
and pick up what's left of my change.
The regulars go their way, I go mine,
slinging over my shoulder one more
'Catch you later,
at *The Boat*.'

I hold a man fortunate who, in the dead of winter,
happens on one of those all-night mead halls
where you bring your own;
where the sun will rein up behind each man
and find him exhausted,
slouched as over oars.

Ah, but for now there is only the salt road,
and the blond joy of sea-legged Vikings
still out raiding the wine shelves
of third-generation America.

Everyone in the suburbs is dancing
in a discotheque under the shopping center;
under new snow;
under a sediment of so many nightfalls
since the wolf.
Where was all this before now?

As the record spins, I feel a fusion
of bone & flesh: the blood tall
on a floor huge with music. Mine only for a night,
this music,—which was always somewhere inside me.

The words of the song have something to do with
the Barbary Coast,
the fishwives shoveling the shells of rebirth.
But the rhythm leads forward,
up shiny ramps of aluminum, to Venus.
Everyone is reaching for the rungs of orbits
that will take them back, in time, to Earth
in its radioactive youth;
back to that golden age of Californium.

Another double for Ray!
the fox-jowled insurance man
crouched at the bar,
guarding another hard-won day
on the circuit: beleaguered,
but asserted by a hunting shirt
beneath his shabby business
suit, worn slick at the seat.

Some people we can spot,
completed faces in the mirror;

and we drink doubly for it.

Summers,
he haunts deer-headed ski resorts,
still looking for a wife at 54,
pine-needled moonlight covered
by a policy of sportsmanship
and old times;

still wondering why his old man,
with all his fine pointers
and leisure,
                    shot himself.

When the raw wind works its branches
at the window, reaching for the cracks
in the dark,
the living room sits very still. What now?
Perhaps it is looking for the leaves
pressed away in old books;
or that pine needle lost since Christmas
in the lining of the overstuffed chair.
One of these days it's going to break in
again,
—only to stand there, boughed with ice,
come to the wrong place after all.

—for Freydis, my spiritual mother

I've been here before, I think, by daylight,
so drunk I thought I was alive again;
after a sitting room of many hands folded, wintering;
or feeling for hard wood under the rug.
Pregnant, much poorer than I,
you swaggered down to the fjords,
past the stone fields, past the old woman's house
with the chicken in back;
not whimpering, or stooping to pick up butts
in the sand. I think of you. And my uncle,
who thought of Vinland only as a place to get drunk.
But the sea gave you your strength,
as you gave those Vikings theirs: insulting them,
putting your own breasts to the sword that time
to scare off the Skraelings . . .
I think of my own hands, the way they give off toxins
from the night before;
and I'm ashamed.
You too had heard of the land of those who yell loudly.
By moonlight, the dragons were there to meet you;
and the dark months just before daybreak
to see you off . . .
But I have no one, just the fog;
and these lowing tugs you would've put to graze someplace
further down the coast . . .
And it's here again, that half-dark
when the warrior retires, without reproach.
But I have never seen those icy sea caves
I was meant to go back to; and the boat is gone.
Soon the sun will come, exposing the city, its women,

their false breasts laid by on window sills;
and viciously, we'll meet to buy another day of time,
secretly expecting to be supplanted.

[20] A BUCKET KICKED ASIDE
IN MEMORY OF THOSE FEW WHO MUST DIE YET
TO MAKE COWARDICE A UNANIMITY

It was a younger man, but a firmer man
who cheered the first entrenchments
of the war.
He & I have been these seven dirty years
taking leave
of one another.
Now it is settled.
My bones are fit for removal.

It is not seemly a man should rend open by day
The huge roots of his blood trees.
                                    —JAMES WRIGHT

                    I

        Give the monkey a wrench;
        let him follow his hands.
        For he was there, also, at the winter's edge.
        Now is ever the moment of improvisation.
        And though I have just come on fresh
        for the night shift, I feel these things:
        the glacial floors led off to drains;
        the westward-digging feet of Irish shepherds,
        that have held up for millennia,
        give out on a gas lot halfway to Buffalo
        in lifting a greasy coffee cup to the moon.
        And you limp on, you brothers to waitresses,
        sons & descendants of Cro-Magnon the hale; —
        cursing like the devil on your fallen arches.
        Dreaming by day of winning back your women
        by night. But no one down here gets any younger.
        You put up with it, pumping the gas, & smiling,
        a little sheepish, with a growl
        from deep in the ropy linings of your stomachs.

        We work at this station because it's here;
        or because our entire lives come down to the shores
        of Erie Boulevard. Some of us cross it.
        Those who do, work for Die-old . . .

II

The room is bare; as deathless
as a windshield is believed to be.
Streetlights, like the sudden bodies of insects,
splash in my vision.
But this is not Mars: one of her canals left unburied,
its spirit to fly free through the red dark.
Not even water rats could chew their way in here,
there's so much glass.—And I go out, nightly,
to the dead float of my race in passing,
into the November of the planet Earth.
It's not seemly, I know.
But how do you linger back
in the strong sweep of headlights,
or hide on the banks of open space?
Outside of the lost, or out of air,
my only comforters are winds
still uncharted, shifting & reshifting the islets
of debris. Strange things,

leaves: now dryads
driven all at once up phone poles;
now oreads
alive & hesitating at the drains
the way a rodent waits
before running in front of an oncoming car.

III

Maybe you've seen me after closing,
still in my Texaco greens,
still flexing an empty beer can,
looking for something I can call a day.
Here's time to unravel that gully of willows
I have watched meander
down through the truck farms & used car graveyards;
time to refix the boundaries of survival, reappraise
the tracks of that Ice Age across my palm.

Not looking, tripping over empty crates, the night
    deepens.
But the death of one snowflake on the lower lip
is not enough to raise the stream that comes,
dry to the hand.
In this valley, there's not one smooth stone in place
to show there ever was a crosscut to the sea.

And here is time to take a last look at Venus,
still a cold green glasjular, just out of reach
in a badge of sky: one breakthrough in the afterbirth
that closes in on us, rejecting light.
This skyless winter is the white man's;
his alone are these moving fields of snowclouds
sooty & trampled-looking
even before their fall.

IV

It gave me a start,
the dawn-ready light of this first snow
fallen on the ground. I haven't slept all night;
yet for certain, I have just been awakened.
And looking into these ghost-clear eyes,
wife,—still you will ask me what I do nights
I don't come home; sometimes make me wonder myself.
Perhaps you too awoke: a redstart or a robin
that called by mistake, once,
after 'last call' at *The Boat,*
then left the house dark.
The curtain breathed slowly,
lifting & falling into dawn
without me . . .

But I am shivering! I'm superstitious with it. Who
is that girl with the doodlebugs for eyes?
Her face is dull, & creased with dirt;
and her hair moves slowly
across the previews of bone.
So this is where it's at: right here all the time.
So *this* is where I am to be laid.

*

And she didn't even know me.
No, it's not that she would let me die there
on the median; it's just that she was scared,
she didn't know how things were for me,
there, underground;
how certain spadesful of the human ditch
had staked their claim on me.

V

And just because we have followed
the woman in the sun
across the hemisphere of winter,
herding the endless glaciers of Eurasian sheep,—
just because we are winter's own,
in sheep's clothing,—
doesn't mean that spring never comes back
to salted ground:
that spring doesn't find me clung like a mollusk
to the curbstone edge of the inevitable.
Comes a thaw, and the poles are once more upon us;
and the air is the very commemoration
of inland seas.
Spilled gasoline runs off in rainbows;
and the oil that has lain embedded
in fissures of ice; and the gravels from other states.
And the snowbanks plowed up wave on wave all winter,
wrought by many winds & stars,
break suddenly, all at once,—
though several million years too late,—
on the silent & receding shores

of Iriquois Lake.

VI

What's this noon sun have to do with my midnight?
How long have the pumps been silent?

Yet the blood is still ticking, booming in fact,
in the blue-black return of the veins.
What else can a man do on his one day off,
but hang around his job with a hangover?
'I just didn't have the midnight in me, man',
said one who quit, snowblind.
You better downshift. It's time,
—o thou shepherd turned sheriff.
So this is what's become of
the men who wore the star.

VII

And when you haven't slept all day,
it disappears over a man-made embankment.
Here, where the gas war has raged now,
full six truckloads & a day, a hard fill falls clean
through the tops of buried maples, into stubble
half-submerged in the dark. Nothing moves
where I looked for the river, the colors of snow
in the woods to my grandmother's house for Thanksgiving;
and the orange I had hoped to get.
I see nothing but gravegrass; and exhaust pipes
coughing the digested dead: the color of my own water
falling, so hot it burns holes in the blackening snow.
Indian winter, that damp shade, is out there someplace:
a proud man asleep in an abandoned car.
But tonight, it's a long way back down to that cornfield
he taught us to plant.
And over in the sheds & family rooms, his nation
will be gathered again, though chiefless,
thankful that I didn't come to dinner this year either.
We burn leaves to each other.
And at stray times, caught between two lanes of traffic,
we look away, pretending to hear canal boats underfoot.
And times are very much the same:
the only thing that feels safe in a hundred acres
is this glacier of oil cans,
and maybe me here thanking Providence

there are still more wolves than cities.

This open wound of winter
somehow warms the blood,
now that the river moves alone
beneath its dark ice.
So long ago the river lost this arm;
and yet, among these reeds, it is still
as if I were fly-casting, bending once more
to unhook some feathers caught on low-riding limbs.
Almost as if I were learning all over again
to be patient: what with the oaks that have gone down
here, trying to break
the flight of the redwing blackbird.

Wake me slowly
from those first cold sheets
of spring,
when the pilot light has been out
all night, and I am still
rambling on
about the orange groves at the city dump.

Now it is afternoon most of the day.
The window lies long & blindered
on the ridged linoleum;
but the glass is cold to the breath.
And the ticks in the floor are asleep
in the direct heat of the sun.
Great wings of snow are being lifted in the sun.
But I just listen to the radiator,
dozing, neither here nor there.

For My Wife, Because I Forgot to Get Her a Valentine

In the wreath of unmelted snow
around a smudgepot
under the New York Central overpass,
I find the words tonight.
I'm sorry.
Any women who were here with me
have gone their own ways
over the years.
Their initials on the walls are repeated
over & over
to themselves.

Midsummer

This morning it is not enough to say
the time of the radish has come & gone
beneath the ground.
At the sight of these besoms,
tops & twigs the earthworms have planted anew
in their tiny dawn exits,—
the straw man smolders inside of me,
leaping in cartwheels after the sunlight
thrown off of high places.
I stand up, a blessing
on all things six foot or under.

GREETING THE FIRST MARCH WIND
WITH A HANGOVER

Awakened by a knock of icicles,
I half-dream of schoolgirls
romping out of pale kingdoms
on bucket feet.

I open the door to a loudness
of crows comparing treetops.

The whistle of a paperboy blows past,
folded into a great wind
of weathered houses,
where nightshirt-women banging breakfast dishes
slowly rub their kitchens warm again.

And something behind me knows
that all the empty bottles of Spain
are content.

O Mars, April comes
to try a dark age;
and you set your last berserker loose.
And so, on the first night wet with robins,
Lenten & venereal, he slouches to the sticks
with his dead tree thrown over one shoulder.
But the needles he sows along the way
do not sprout the delirious skeletons
with swords. He knows this
without looking back.
And he feels your winds falling dead
drunk, on the hilts of broken bottles
sunk in dying shapes of snow.

My head aches noiselessly,
no longer caring where I step;
in the fresh-turned furrows, or their shadows.
And my face, your face, is impotent with rage,
washing away the blood
with blood. I sweat, caught red-handed;
bark hands fumbling with small seeds
in the heat of the moon.
The net that falls for you is soft & shredded.
It is the breath of babies being reassured
in the nesting dark; the old dark;
the tinsel's new branches. Merry Xmas.

Floods were serious things in the north woods.
Sometimes late at night, my father & some men
would be laughing over ale in a rough room
that lumbered out over
one side of a ravine,
overhearing the river.
Away from wind or wife,
the ash of a cigarette would lean a long way down
before falling, so immersed they'd be.
And forty feet below the joke,
the vast schools & timbers
passed each other in silence
through the melting night.
You could almost see the hole sawed through the icy air
by the gaslight, when one of them
would lift the trap door up
to toss down a can.
And I tell you: this is when they'd laugh loudest.
You see, there was always the river's laugh
drowning them out.

Just now it has struck me.
A hearse careens into the intersection,
grinding its gears: full of kids
on their way to another bar.
And right in the path of its headlights,
I see shiny things . . . worms.

I can feel them, each with four hearts,
threading the new grass underfoot.
Spring breathes me in again.
How quick they are to draw back,
inching Earth its first real notch up from

the hemisphere of water.

She's a long way off yet,
looking in the field from side to side.
Nothing bolts from dead grass
sheafed & knotted by the snows,
though she searches scythelike.
But then, it could've been herself
crouched in hiding there, ready to spring:
something conscious, a loose knot slipping down
on the ankles of the wind. Who is she,
thus turned out of doors,—or never brought in?
And the barn: did it tilt too far; or did it burn
and move noiselessly on, just out of earshot?
Black drifts say nothing where they fatten here,
and fall away from one man's first harvest
of stones. And what of me?
If I give myself up to returning grass;
if my hands are thatched over my eyes,
can I be the cottage she glimed at?
the reaper she hid from in the darkrise of heads
uncut at fences? Look how boldly she roots there now,
where winds slow barely long enough for old footpaths
& quickening waters.
Maiden or Mother, there's no rest for you, I guess,
in all of heathendom . . .

A window must've flickered somewhere
in the first warmth of shadows behind me.
She has seen that the field ends
sooner than she had expected.
It must be me: now she's running;
she has something to ask me.

"Did you find a key?"

(One superstition associated with salt fish was that if a 'dream line,' the strip in the center, was eaten before going to bed, a girl or a young man would see in a vision her or his future marital partner handing out a glass of water.)

At times I can almost see her.
Often she has just finished crying,
or taking a bath; whose early widow
leans over a wall of her own hair,
a thousand miles or so east of nightfall,
and cups the hallway empty to her face?
Her back is turned. I can hear nameless feet
falling up long stairwells of exposed root,
now finding them the same, now utterly lost
in spring blizzards of maple seeds
following a rain. Long past now,
and yet I am looking right into those dark pools
caught in the knuckles,
where they can't be absorbed;
can't even be taken by swallows,
or clouds drifting forty feet down.
This water has stood so long; and still
it is far from finished pouring.

And the seeing-eye dogs of the moon are out
barking at underground rivers;
snapping at the blind hands
that reach, between damp pillows, for a window
left open once a year.
And it has all been prepared for me,
those blackened anniversaries of her blonde face
that have yearly mourned for me in secret.
And the silence.
And the breastless Void.

If they are really birds that call here,
they have eyes that are older than bone;
and their throats are forever ragged
with the dampfall just after a rain.
For these are birds that know the moss hollows,
and the silence of dead trees that stand a long time
before slipping, at last, in the fog.
The branches here come down so far,
they glide right by you
on wings of black leaves
put back by the rising waters.

Even so, you must let the stream take you
around its dark bends.
It has something to show you,
though it doesn't look back at you with riffles.
This is the kind of stream that has no name,
that never panics on long journeys underground.
It's all right: long before it thinks of bogging down,
it lets its birds go
to river the human skies northward.
For this is a wood in migration;
a wood that stays wild but a day sometimes,
pitched on some farmer's back forty;
or wherever you first overheard
the true calls of birds.

It was hardly a path,
in my headlights;
and it vanished beneath a honeysuckle bush,
where the fence posts of two ancient lots
came together, at dusk.
And tacked no more than inches off the ground,
a faded circus poster lit up like a doorway
on the green air just before spring.

When I rolled down my window to look,
I heard faint cries: children's voices
still out playing
far from get-home-to-supper America.
Small buds hesitated all around me,
faery spittle on the dark.
Somewhere a door closed.
And it was going to sprinkle.

Whatever it was that had led me there
was gone forever, in another day.
Yet you still see them scooting
across the road,—the same road you all take
to what's-its-name.
Just on the way there myself,
when I made up my mind to drive on
to the end of the world.

WORDS ENTRUSTED TO THE FLANKS OF A WHITE DOE
I ALMOST HIT WHERE THREE ROADS MEET
NEAR DELPHI, N. Y.

The gaunt moon of daytime will speak for me
in higher courts of April;
this is where I turn.
Again I cannot light out on my own.
Though my paunch falls, ripe with the dews
of fruitless winter drunks,—I'm not ready
for midsummer's padded cell . . .

So many years, my wife has doodled by the phone.
She was never of the wild hair & rootless ways
I had imagined.
Even fully grown,
my brothers dream of astronauts
afloat in amniotic seas.
How long must a first-born
be a father to his kind?
I have sat too long with my father's staff,
left hanging in the cellar with its tale
of robbers. It wouldn't lie, and yet
I find myself alone
with the riddle of two-leggedness.

The old car limps homeward,
high on mirages, high on the good times gone bad.
And churches, half-animal
in the hood-heat of the suburbs,
go on eating my city's corpses
as they come along. And every day,
under the same bridge, I see this blind man
drinking rotgut from a paper bag.

Now what does he know?
—or I, of depression:
except that the god of unfrosted light bulbs
stalks us in an unmarked car.

But I survive.
No kings are killed here.
No teeth knocked loose by the bishop's confirming blow.
All the entrails read 'Inspected, Number such & such.'
I hear the wind sometimes; but I know
the falling candelabra will be saved, as always,
by the cord . . .

*

You run along now, in the antler-growing season;
find your ancient southeast passage to the sea.
Keep off of roads. And dare me
with that day,
beyond beast & bramble,
when I will cut myself a staff for those mountains.

Where do they go, who stretch their legs here after lunch?
Back inside the factory,
into the cinder beds of their own shadows.

You have to walk fast to keep up with railroad ties.
And you have to learn to listen
with the bones at the back of your head.

Rails so long & straight, they lead practically nowhere,
blind boxcar after boxcar,
into a distance the shape of dying sound.

You have to stretch your legs pretty far
to get to Pogo Pogo;
like tracking a ghost train lost high in the mountains.

O the bums of Pogo Pogo, when they beg,
slump holding the pans of their brains.
When a job involves mud, they cross one leg;
the other they cross when it rains.

If I knew for a certainty that a man was coming
to my house with the conscious design of doing me
good, I should run for my life . . .
                          —THOREAU

I

Each day, each working day in winter
throbbing like a bloodmobile
around the corner from another war;
each day my door hangs in a block fence
pending demolition
in the stockyards of the poor;
each day I live dying: I swear
I'm getting out of here!
But the circuits in the walls run on & on.
It is a hibernation of all sense,
when there is no emotion; only time
outside falling, but never reaching the ground
for sure: when it's better to cross your legs
to sleep, feel the cold sands creeping up in you
with less reason to move than ever before.
It's a time when men dream of spring & rebirth,
and the Man who will buy their bodies for research.

II

I should've been a black bear
on its last cross-country feed.
An old bear, that knew of a cave
still undynamited;
living off the dumps & public places,
walking flat-foot through fire
with eyes that shine in the dark.

Though I land on death row for my lot,
I'll take my Chances;
this is how I win: passing GO, collecting my $200.
Inside, I know there's no reprieve for a dying city,
or a dying sun.
So I'll walk that mile of numbered hairs
I'd like to leave behind me when I die.

III

Getting out of jail free in Syracuse, N. Y.,
I see strange signs on sticks;
light beards & dark glasses; people
who are Greek to me.
But then, I shall be carried home on my lean-to,
my pole beans still flying the red moon
of planting. Home to my storm in the sun
I shall somehow be carried, a three-time loser.
If I falter at the edges of the park,
it's not just to look at the map.
For when all roads lead to Washington, you know
why those endless white obelisks
He's strung along the highways of the world.
And when your body's not your own,
you understand His sacred cattle
bussed like gladiators
to the slave docks of their birth.
And leaving a home in the Empire State,
there is no place to go but Home.

IV

Near the ampitheatre in Thornden Park,
in the shade dug under the stage entrance,
there is a quiet spot
where one south-side tavern maid was raped:
chased with a tire iron; trees & fence posts blazed
with car paint. She dashed for these very same firs;
thought she'd step out, in defiance of the Rose Queens;
do her death leap in front of a congressional silence
of crickets. Still reaching, the chance moon found her,
just yards from the gate: locked,
with A-frame reinforcements
where the bars had been tried already.
A tight squeeze it would've been anyway,
though naked, for all she had drunk.
I remember her blood on the sneakers
some hoods were showing off at the ice cream parlor;
and the human chains of policemen
combing the brush for her belongings
next day. Never found. Conjectures,
down on all fours: just give me a pine cone,
and I'll make a speech . . .

Time,
time is all I need: just a handful of time
to be kind
to the lint in my pockets.

Summer tires sing to us on long trips;
voices that are just behind the heat
when the sun is drawing low.
It is the watery sun
that follows you on ahead,
squinting cold through the slats
of abandoned barns: its hints
of the life that goes on, of the woman
in the sun—who waits for us
after the harvests of the planets,
after the grey farms, the waters gone rusty,
and the horsehair snakes
for which all men are homesick.

It is August.
It is too late in the earth
to recover many sections
of the pipe.
It seems we may soon have to face the hard fact
of animal heat.

For some time now,
this girl on horseback has been watching us drill
from a distance. She turns
in the shade of a forked elm, then slowly dips
into a field
our instruments have steered us away from.

This place is haunted
by the chance of meeting you:

the wave stems of your hair,
the deep green fathoms & positions
of your eyes;
the gull flight of your lost smile.

My breath still quickens a stroke
when I think of the undersea bowers
of your clasped arms, so long ago.

And the caudal crossing of your bare feet.
And your knees, your imbricated knees.

I still feel lonely where you left me
mopping out the water closet, as it were.

Look for me in country stores
abandoned for their wood.
Still hear me rapping
out back. It is summer
in the deep tombstone shadow
of the Texaco pump
leaning dry in the doorway.

Many Friday nights, in many small towns
this past summer, many farmers' daughters
tired of traveling salesmen
tied their older brothers' shirt tails
up in knots beneath their breasts.
And slipping out to meet boys their age
under streetlamps, their midriffs
were something all their own,
with their hands in back pockets
of blue jeans: fading away
from screened porches in the dark,
in all directions of the fireflies
of many fading territories,
this past summer.

Getting into an old car
parked in the mountains,
you feel as if you were a troll
crouched underneath a bridge.
The car is still yours;
but you've been in the woods so long,
it's like the inside of a man's face
staring absently off through the rain
with fogged glasses, just before dusk.
The charred stones of the engine are quiet.
And you see it's the cold that's important,
the mouths of caves high in mountains.

What is it a September dawn finds
left standing in the flue of night,
that keeps men occupied indoors
another hour of the hemisphere,
though no one has slept?
It is the night light
by which the air was out hunting the fields.
It is a road lamp still on,
but not rushing to warm itself at the windows
of the overheated house.

And the stream that was lifted from the culvert
is on course, and still high
on the footholds of message poles;
bare trees no longer governed by night & day.
And yet autumn came this close to earth
last night. This cricket just told me,
—the late one, that gives out the long wail
from deep in the subversive forests
of the grass.

The pear tree, in the backyards of cities,
is like a plant that survived the Flood.
To see one is to suddenly look up
and catch sight of a great northern pike
in the daytime, in a downtown bar.
Both have that skin of the survivor.

But a pear tree on an abandoned farm
is like a great-aunt gone broke,
and forced to live with in-laws in the suburbs.
After dances in strange gardens with gazeboes,
those women are old now, and live next door
with lace-covered shade pulls in the windows.

Clotheslines find their way into pear trees,
and bent nails; but never any children.
So their leaves, in the fall do not lie easily.
You hear them well into January thaw,
—almost as if still trying to attract a partridge
in this darkened world.

It happens all at once
one morning in October.
The crickets you still hear
have been silent for weeks.
The leaves have come down for good.
It is the hour when the ribs of pumpkins
first get their gold. It is that moment
when the cupolas of haunted houses,
their windows already dulled by interior fogs
of age, begin the long crossing
of winter.

All afternoon, you watch a fine snow fall
without a sound, or a trace of white.
As the crowded faces in the clouds pass over,
dreaming in their sleep, you see it is a snow
that was always falling in the coming dark.
A snow filled with dust, & the sounds of insects;
and warm nights sinking away, at one
with the moving molecules of a bedpost.

But here in this field, it is an unlikely snow;
an exile of voices in tangled frequencies
strayed down from cities of the all-night air.
Lonely voices, that have fallen great distances
only to fall away now, down furrows, past clods
all headed for the same house, which is dark.
Or if they are heard, it is only in passing;
particles of static fallen from a white sound.

I

You can get lost now,
and be glad to have been called 'mother.'
Of late I have learned that the leaves fall
as of old:
some dampen, and turn into fish;
but many hasten away in time
to be birds.

II

Now let's see, right about here
we could use one: something slow,
that doesn't shed a lot,—to set off the yellow
of the brick;
you know:
something to sit down and strip off your tie under,
after you've just been fired
at fifty.

III

When they had the ancestry dug up;
one, a president, found himself
a trickle of root embedded
in the huge stone
of his name.
Broken off at the point of entering that white house,
his skull,
he saw those last years flicker:

one drop of water enshrined the floors
of unfamiliar seas.

IV

And who is to pity those Xmas trees
rolled tumbling by March winds
through the ghost towns
of innercity?

Just once I'd like to climb up
on that longhorn out front.
But then, it's old; it hasn't long to go.
Maybe five or six to a thousand.
And its shed, since July, burnt orange
on the ground.

Then I'll sit at its foot.
And even after they've dehorned it, I stay on,
clung like a locust shell in the cleavage
of that great hoof;
watching long avenues of its dying brothers,
the Americans,
find their way safely home
to November.

I

It is just before daybreak in Constableville.
Pieces of the great pumpkin lie in the road.
The Yankee village hid its face all summer,
moving daily through the scattered fields;
and was suddenly transported.

They straggled off after the snake dance,
and left tissue paper snarled in the trees;
trembling in prickers along the cemetery fence;
and in the dead grass, rolling over & over
without eyes.

Only now in my headlights do dummies surprise me;
and those bare trees fly up in the darkness,
cold as a witch's bloodstream, and mysterious
as a man on his way early to a milk shed.

II

Because I have never seen the Black River,
it is all around me, like a humor.
It is the sound of the wind
through my butterfly window;
it is a flow we inherit driving north all night
through isolated pastures,
where the stone pates of buried mountains
surface in the wind.
It's a river you wouldn't know in the daylight,
on All Saints' Day.

Older trout climb hard
to make a hill like this.
One must be accurate in feeders,
laying, leaping for that last pool, only
to be seen no more.

Secret spots,
where spring has gone back
into the ground.
It's the little things that settle: a hook,
or a crawdad's grindstone,
smooth on a bed of metals & salts
behind a root.
Only ten per cent of a fishing body
ever thinks to come here.

Unnoticed, I step between two spawning rainbows.
Knee-deep in low branches
laden with autumn leaves,
the rest of me rushes back downhill,
as it will have to do again someday
when I die.

Just a speck is all you'll see of yourselves
before the morning moon fills up with water,
and is gone;
calling back, you will hear this soft music
piped up from the spirits' vault of Earth.

The rooms all vacant and vague
The east wall beats on the west wall
At the center nothing.

— HAN-SHAN
(translated by Gary Snyder)

Now in all directions of the goldenrod,
it is winter again. The briar hoops are bare.
And the secret passageways of boyhood
are all mapped with snow,
that once closed of themselves behind me
with leaves. No use enlarging a womb
I have outgrown.

How is it with you?
Somewhere down in that valley
of long-faced fires & dust-red summers,
hidden in the hollow of a stick of bamboo
by the kitchen door,
my leftovers will be waiting for me still,
I guess. So I've saved you this gall, Shite,
hoping you might not call me crazy, and mean it.
No servants' quarters—this spare room that bulges
on the axis of the cold; this, my narrowest escape
from those madmen you cook for.
Hah! And who scatters more burrs than I do
on my way home drunk, taking the longcuts, always;
even through my own backyard.